Autumn Clears

Autumn Clears

Poems by

Jane Edna Mohler

© 2025 Jane Edna Mohler. All rights reserved.
This material may not be reproduced in any form, published,
reprinted, recorded, performed, broadcast,
rewritten, or redistributed without
the explicit permission of Jane Edna Mohler.
All such actions are strictly prohibited by law.

Cover design by Shay Culligan
Cover art and design by Peter Stolvoort
Author photo by Peter Stolvoort

ISBN: 978-1-63980-747-5
Library of Congress Control Number: 2025937831

Kelsay Books
502 South 1040 East, A-119
American Fork, Utah 84003
Kelsaybooks.com

for the love and verve of my husband Peter,

for the many times my son James says, "Same,"

and for the memory of my father, a quiet and ardent gardener

Acknowledgments

The author wishes to express her gratitude to these journals and their busy editors for publishing these poems.

A Certain Kind of Swagger (anthology): "The Speaking of Trees"
American Journal of Poetry: "Dead Man's Dessert," "When I Think About Herons"
Bay to Ocean Journal: "Hanging on the Gates," "Every Tuesday Morning," "Feral Apples," "The Names Remain Unspoken," "Did You Pause?" "Corn at Market"
Bucks County Herald: "November Reckons" (reprint)
Eastern Shore Writers' Association, Crossroads Contest, 2nd place: "Corn at Market"
Gargoyle: "Making Friends in the Pandemic," "Spectators," "Miserere," "Leftover"
Gyroscope: "The Strays of Incheon"
MacQueen's Quinterly: "November Reckons," "Open House," "Unstoppable," "Quiet!"
New Verse News: "Drill," "Rouh"
ONE ART: a journal of poetry: "Dad Had Levels," "Feast," "A Stone's Story," "Forbidden Colors," "Mortal Lessons," "Rare Beasts," "Ornithology Lessons," "She's Always Hungry," "Fences Take"
Quartet: "'Bringing in the Sheaves'"
River Heron Review: "Circling," "What It Is I Fear"
Schuylkill Valley Journal: "Day Keeping," "Did You Pause?" (reprint)
Sheila-Na-Gig: "At the Foot of the Bridge"
U.S.1 Worksheets: "What Not to Cut," "The Widower," "Write to Me"
Verse-Virtual: (all reprints) "Corn at Market," "The Strays of Incheon," "What It Is I Fear"

The author expresses deep gratitude for the support and editorial wisdom of Cheryl Baldi, poet, editor, and dear friend.

She is grateful to her lifelong friend, Barbara Strigel, for the many decades of sharing literature, critical reading, artistic support, and collaboration with her photography.

She is indebted to her writing teachers: R. Gerry Fabian, Martha Collins, and the late Christopher Bursk.

She extends her gratitude for the fellowship and support of the Bucks County poetry community, founded and nurtured by Chris Bursk.

Thanks also go to the brackish members of the Eastern Shore Writers' Association led by a most generous poet, Tara A. Elliott.

She sends gratitude to Karen Kelsay and her meticulous staff at Kelsay Books.

Above all, she sends bushels of love to Peter for his support and belief in her work, and to James for making her his mother and helping her understand a few things about herself.

Contents

A Stone's Story   17

1. loaded with ghosts

Ghost Ghazal   21
At the Foot of the Bridge   22
Dead Man's Dessert   23
When I Think About Herons (1)   24
Quiet!   25
Dad Had Levels   26
Dream: Two Commas   27
A Choice Ring   28
Ornithology Lessons   29
When I Think About Herons (2)   30
Four Magpies   31
Every Tuesday Morning   32
Crusty   33
Patience and Fortitude   34
Miserere   35
Longing Itself Brings the Cure   36
The Strays of Incheon   37

2. the patient dark

The Speaking of Trees   41
Day Keeping (2020)   42
Making Friends in the Pandemic   43
Spectators   44
Circling   45
Drill   46
Rouh   47

One of Us Has to Go in Alone	48
A Conspiracy	50
Stroop Waffles	51
The Widower	52
Open House	53
Leftover	54
Dream: Common Crops	55
The Names Remain Unspoken	56
Did You Pause?	57
What It Is I Fear	58

3. prepare

Longevity	63
"Bringing in the Sheaves"	65
Hanging on the Gates	66
The Blue Jay	67
Forbidden Colors	68
Rare Beasts	70
Fences Take	72
Unstoppable	73
As One	74
Mortal Lessons	75
Feral Apples	76
What Not to Cut	78
Feast	79
Corn at Market	80
Love Letter to My Garden	82
Sweetness	83
Write to Me	84
November Reckons	85
She's Always Hungry	86

Mono no aware (物の哀れ) Japanese idiom:
The awareness of the transience of all things
heightens the appreciation of their beauty
and evokes a gentle sadness at their passing.

—Wikipedia

A Stone's Story

I was a hunk
of rock you could barely
lift without grunting.

Remember that hot beam glaring
from my core? I shivered
a fever you'd give your right hand

to feel. That white degree.
I pulsed through the earth's sharp
shell, or did I plunge

from a wrathful sky?
No matter.
It's the story that counts.

I was all you'd expect
from a god, not the dull stone
you think you see.

That wasn't me, folded
into the warm row of a tilled field,
the comfort of worms as neighbors.

Not me spending decades mired
in mud, scored by the blade
of a brainless plow.

1

loaded with ghosts

Ghost Ghazal

My parents' house, its pursed lips, loaded with ghosts.
Sold last week, even the orchard glows with ghosts.

Past Halloweens, my serious son: ninja, Zorro, vampire.
Holidays split two ways. Bins of photos coded with ghosts.

Out front, an early commute, cars line up at the stop signs.
Some honk and curse. Most are goaded by ghosts.

Picking up take-out, a girl at the bar wears a worried smile.
Scared to be home alone, her bed is soaked with ghosts.

Lenape took the creek by my home as a road to theirs.
Crayfish witness its banks eroded by ghosts.

Fishing boat covered, firewood stacked, beds of thistle,
and a new cat grave. Autumn day owned by ghosts.

Scour with vinegar and a stern wire brush, hard
work to smooth this poet corroded by ghosts.

At the Foot of the Bridge

      Nothing's slicker
than a midnight burger blasted
down in my father's Ford.

      All-night drive-in, lurid
lights hum over the hot macadam
salted with skittering rats.

      Wrappers rattle. Whoosh
of invisible cars, their black speed stirs
a wind sopping

      like a stale sponge.
Night smeared with the smoke
of seared meat.

      We think our own
thoughts wrapped in darkness
thick as bay water.

      Eight-years old, I fell
for the lure of night rides, inherited
that craving for neon-splashed

      hours when Fryolators
hoist a greasy tower that billows
in the faces of wide-eyed stars.

Dead Man's Dessert

We called shoo fly pie dead man's dessert.
Always served it at funerals. Coming home
he smelled the cinnamon and molasses baking,
and the carcass of a deer in the back field.

Always served it at funerals. Coming home
after years at war, everything was new,
except the carcass of a deer in the back field.
He didn't want anyone to know he returned.

After years at war everything was new except
matted brown leaves entrenched in the gutters.
He didn't want anyone to know he returned
home, where he can finally close his eyes.

Matted brown leaves entrenched in the gutters.
He smelled the cinnamon and molasses baking.
Home where he can finally close his eyes.
We called shoo fly pie dead man's dessert.

When I Think About Herons (1)

I don't like to think
about Mother crashing
through her last years.
Those bloody gashes
furniture left
on her thin legs.
In the end, her skin
was dark as leather.
Her brown teeth bit
for nearly a century.
Unlike the heron,
she wanted people close,
all the better to hunt,
to jab for bits of them
like plain minnows.
Her plans weren't simple,
always an angle, a feint.
In the end she had
no element.

Quiet!

As a kid, I used a Ouija board
to scratch the surface
of the beyond. I craved

conversation. Mother used
it as a desk blotter.
She paid

bills over that field,
ignoring the lonely
spirit who tried

to speak. Now I keep
that old board buried
in the closet.

I can't talk about Mother
anymore. I worry
she might hear.

Dad Had Levels

Some say death is the great equalizer.
Sam Colt claimed it was his forty-five
caliber Peacemaker. Dad had tools.

Dirt crumb by dirt crumb, he labored,
his heavy oak level grading a perfect
slant beside our home.

Even then its wood was serious,
dark as barn plank.
Dad liked to make things line up.

Now his Sears Torpedo Level gleams,
its small bubble still directing
perfection from inside an amber tube.

I keep his cement trowel too, blackened
steel, the worn handle smoked with time.
Dad wanted everything smooth.

These tools rest beside red pens and my
pica rule from a typesetting job, where daily
I made nearly invisible adjustments to type.

Dream: Two Commas

There was nothing but two commas, two together
with nothing in between. No words!
And nothing I could do, hogtied
in another bang-my-head-against-the-wall dream.

I squirmed, longed to remove one comma, or fill
the pair with a witty aside, a pithy omniscience.
Poets and therapists love dreams. They guarantee
filling a page, or the fifty-minute hour. But punctuation?

That's what draws the eye of my subconscious?

Decades ago, on my first day as a typesetter,
I left off the last letter of a dead socialite's
name. One tacked-on "e," unnecessary
and bothersome as the blank in my dream.

In 30 pt Palatino my error remains, and so do I.

But now those mental faults and blanks multiply.
Commas go rogue. Minds of their own.
What was that elusive phrase that refused
to appear? A sin of omission?

The aphasia of aging and heaped up
bad decisions? Maybe home truths
too wounding to know, all whisked
away before I could see.

A Choice Ring

The slender band lay jostled
with orphaned earrings, souvenir
paste, and the tangled

chains of Mother's jumble.
Peeking inside, I found
the maker's stamp, *CHOICE,*

my father's initials, and a date
in March when my mother
was nearly four.

Then I read the initials
of my father's first wife
whose ring has come to me

by hard feelings and odd luck.
I've heard stories whispered
about that young wife.

Slurs no different
than what has been said about me.
I know the weight of choices,

the dry throat of saying
what busts up a thing,
those crashing dishes.

I wear her ring.

Ornithology Lessons

My yard ripples
with blue jays, a throng
of little tyrannosaurs

screeching and shuffling
seed. Before consulting
Peterson's, I offered

apple and peach parings.
All spurned. Now I know
those jays want berries.

Is it a trivial thing to learn
what pleases
another?

*

Whenever Mother deemed
some effort worthless,
she'd wave an arm and say,
That's for the birds.

With no propensity for parenting,
cowbirds leave their eggs
to the care of others. Yet
how those fledglings

strut, it's all
sweet feed
and what's right
now.

When I Think About Herons (2)

I like to think about herons,
those gangly Great Blues;
how they move decisively.
I like their elder presence,
they hunt, watch,
and complain
when I come too close.

Once I held an injured hen.
Her sturdy and fragile
body felt hollow, but filled
with something I can't explain.

Herons land by plan,
no plops or splashes,
no disturbance.
They join water,
an element they traverse
as confidently as air.

Four Magpies

One for sorrow, Two for joy,
Three for a girl, Four for a boy . . .
                —Nursery Rhyme

In the thrift store, I cradle a cast-off doll,
smooth the pages of a shy ornithology book.
There's a half-skein of yarn that needs rescuing.

At market, I buy a clutch of butter potatoes, jug
of milk, chunk of cod, and a box of salt.
And always, always a little something extra.

Home, I cross the thin road, cringe on the shoulder
to take in what's left in my crooked mailbox.
I follow someone's steps into the weary

field to retrieve a frozen and mud-soaked
muffler. Grandmother's turkey platter,
Dad's cracked signet ring, and a salt-crusted

surf caster rest easy here. I visit closets, search
for my son's frayed sweater to hold to my face.
I tuck it into the small bed of a drawer.

Won't you come home with me to nest and wait
until once again, there are four.

Every Tuesday Morning

—for James in Korea

I drive a simple road past waking fields.
In October, waves of dry corn tassels soak up
the pink sunrise and glow thick as sable brushes.

But now the fields are cropped, shabby
with November. Warm mornings, a sturdy herd
of Angus head out early; they meet me

with their silent black gaze. When morning is cold
and stiff, they are far off on the horizon, just leaving
the barn in a blue train of steaming muzzles.

I send photos to you each week, certain
you examine that distant
clan under the ever-changing sky.

The sky is always changing.

I hope this unnamed herd matters to you.
That there is something we both look for
every Tuesday morning.

Crusty

—Nantucket Island

It's a muted kind of friendly,
like that one-finger wave from a steering wheel.

Quaise marsh is always crusty.

All winter she wears a stiff shell of salt
and ice. Clods of snow and cedars scratch

her shoulders hunched up against
the wind. Chunks of the hard bay press

yellow-green and stubborn. Brooding
clouds are constantly crowded

by oblivious, party-pink sunrises while
scallops snap and eels nap in the mud.

Quaise marsh will always give you space.

I often think I shouldn't have left.
I had no theory of adhesion,

thought sticking was a talent,
better left to mussels.

Patience and Fortitude

> —Patience *and* Fortitude *are the names of the New York Public Library's marble lions.*

Stores go dark as New Year's Eve looms.
It's probably too late

to get she needs.
On the next barstool a man stares

at the steamy window. He can't see
a thing. He interrupts

her review of tepid resolutions, bets
she might go home with him

once he explains a few things.

*We should go someplace where the music
isn't so loud, somewhere we can talk.*

Harried starlings hurry
from Bryant Park, sifting

through its trees. Invasives,
they foul

the library steps, chatter
their hungers at stone lions.

Miserere

*You desired that truth be in the hidden places,
and in the concealed part You teach me wisdom.*
—Psalm 51

His deep-set eyes looked Russian.
All I can say is those strong roots
in his face made me stare.

> Now, I worship on a floor with one mismatched tile.
> Swaying to psalms, I take note of the shoes around me.

He was young and interested in something
I had said; I can't remember what.
It was a dream, and I didn't need to ask.

> I want to take my fingers and pick at that tile until it gives.
> I want to take it home.

Longing Itself Brings the Cure

—Rumi

Datura yawns,
releasing its night magic.

It's then when my moon recites
Rumi with his face full

upon me. His dark eyes.
His face scarred

because he too is old.
His voice reaches

over the windowsill that holds
me in. He whispers

just one poem, then sends me
back to my beloved.

I don't wonder where he goes.
We never touch. He coaxes

the seas and all that flows.
This may be enough.

The Strays of Incheon

At 2 a.m. Korea time, my son roams the streets carrying
treats for stray cats. They run to him weaving through his legs.

He wanders before returning to his single room sewed
into a slim alley crisscrossed by wires.

It's morning here when he calls, rants about the faults
and obligations of his world. I stay quiet.

I don't know where he's going
but I'm sure he isn't calling for directions.

His city cools, sloughs off days of tramping feet
and roaring motorbikes delivering bibimbap.

He sends video of a cat the neighbors call Little Miss Flower.
She darts from under a Hyundai plastered with emojis.

Unattached, they meet between the streetlights, breathing
the easy darkness.

But couldn't he do this someplace closer?

Then I remember a similar distance, and how it opened
a late-night knowledge that still comes running to me.

2

the patient dark

The Speaking of Trees

You need to stop talking for a while to hear
the voices of trees, the lilt, the slip of leaves
as butter knives spreading thick summer air.

Oaks, ash, and pines speak the same language
having reasoned early on that words unite,
and their accents deepen their discourse.

News of drought or danger is sent by hormones
and electricity, like telegraphs from root to root,
a hum that moles hear instead of wind or waves.

Young trees talk incessantly about green, curled
or jagged edges, veins gorged with slippery juice.
They grumble about the shadows others cast.

Spruce and firs drape dull blue shawls off
their shoulders, speak in motherly shushes
as they sew nearly silent messages into the sky.

Old trees, stingy with their words, whisper high
secrets only hawks can hear. Proud of their rank,
they're content, heedless of their roots' rigid peril.

Day Keeping (2020)

This apron lifts over my head
and ties behind my back. My hands know
where to go. It's part of me now.

Warm water, blue sponge, I bathe
each slippery dish, spoons, cups. Watch
the suds slide off with the rinse.

Stacking has its sense, by heft, size,
and fit in the rack. No different than the slip
of a book into a crowded shelf.

Wine glasses and a crystal vase, dried
with a soft linen cloth. I shine them, rest
them in a high silent place.

Last, the counter, stroked
as a smooth cat.
This prayer,

a keeping
of uncertain days,
no more repetitive than the sun.

Making Friends in the Pandemic

I joined a book club.
Thought we'd talk online,
ease into things.

But they're anxious to eye me up,
want to meet me
on their perfect green lawn,

introduce me to Yama,
Malak Almawt, Samael,
Sareil, Santa Muerte.

I'm the only Jane.
They want to hand me a long cold drink
and smile.

Spectators

Turkey buzzards patrol my neighborhood
twice daily, like cops.

Between rounds, dozens were regular fans
of the local Little League. Pensive,

they studied the games, never yelled,
behaved like bored old men with cheap seats.

Steps were taken. This steady watch
was way too much for parents.

Now these carrion crows haunt the roofline
of the strip mall: five above the pet store,

six over the burger joint, and a dozen sniffing
fumes from *Suzie's Nail Salon.*

Noting unsteady toddlers, they appraise
how tender the puppies might be,

consider the consequences of red meat,
and the beauty of their next meal.

Circling

On a raw stump, far back behind the house,
we offered the quiet gray heart and curled
purple neck of the Christmas turkey.

In the hard cold, the hill crackled underfoot,
and stiff branches tinked like tin
above the soft, blood-scented gift.

Now, deep into January, dark Christmas lights
swing idly from the bare stick bushes.
The stove roars and still the house is chilled.

Gathering wood from the far pile,
convinced of certain suffering, we leave
dog food and table scraps on the stump.

In the crusted snow we find trails
of clawed tracks circling our home,
closer each night.

Our tabbies thread behind the curtains
their pupils wide, staring out
into the patient dark.

Drill

After an armed assailant drill, emotional or physical reactions can be delayed following a highly intense simulation drill.
—National Association of School Psychologists

In the confident glow
of an iPhone, I pass
a silent hour in the school's
utility room with dead
beetles, frantic
spiders, and the librarian
browsing Pinterest.

Pressed against a door
that won't lock, I feel the cold
metal on my back. I brace
one foot on the railing
leading down to oblivious
motors and sweating pipes
accustomed to the peace
of working alone.

The librarian scrolls fervently.
Which chicken recipe
will she choose? Maybe
Easter-themed cupcakes
or a floral wreath crafted
for a family gathering, if
those gunshots we hear are real.

Rouh

—Arabic for "soul"

You were red and blind as a just-hatched robin
when they cut you from your silent mother.

On the news, your curled form was cradled
by a doctor who needed you to live

even more than me. I hope
your nakedness didn't shame you.

It made me love you.

They named you *Rouh,* prescient,
as you had too much soul for the three pounds

your mother had time to give you.
Her name was Sabreen.

They call her a martyr.
You call her Mama.

At five days old you still knew the cadence
of her heartbeat. You flew to her

while your bodies rest under the mud of sorrow
that blood has made of Gaza's dust.

One of Us Has to Go in Alone

Evening in the pandemic hospital sounds
like church on Monday morning.

TVs that usually blast
at the sick beds are silent.

Mother can't or won't talk.
I ask a nurse, *What do I say?*

I text a friend who tells me to kiss
her, and I do, on the forehead.

I didn't like it. And I don't remember
either of us ever doing that. But it's done.

Downstairs the receptionist takes my tag
and asks, *Will I see you tomorrow?*

*

Now the empty roads are iced.
We stop beside the frozen lake, and

I push my head out the car's window
to smell the crystalline gusts. Most geese

have turned in but a few honk quietly
as if they're passing bread between them.

My husband waits until I ask
You'll scatter me here, right? He nods.

You want to be here too? He nods.
Now we have half a plan, but

a plan like this will need a third.
We'll need to find an accomplice.

A Conspiracy

Stealth fit for a burglar,
my neighbor, that fool, loiters
at the elevator shaft.

We don't speak of it.

He's there each evening to steal
the scent of pork and beans that fills
the bellies upstairs.

They're loud.
We both know their messy
mouths are wide open.

He doesn't hunger for their meal.

He hungers for the sugared
air that wafts
from four gathered at one table.

I wouldn't refuse a morsel of that myself.

Stroop Waffles

—for Peter

It begins with stroop waffles, a splurge,
a Christmas treat back in Haarlem, a sacrament,
just one, the elders laid on your tongue.

Then you were off, escaping
the upstairs kids who always had more
able-fisted brothers. You kept

time by passing barges. Hanging
from that one cold bridge, aiming to spit
on a waterman's head, hooting

at his guttural curses. You ruled
that moment when no hand could reach
high enough to smack you.

Now we have tall boxes of *waffelje,*
indulgences of caramel from Costco.
You devour them as if you're catching up

for that red-headed boy coming home
with chapped cheeks, hoping for more
sweetness than you found.

The Widower

—for Jeff

You were thrilled, the garden had slept
as death, until spring spread a pulsing
emerald blanket on the ground.

*It's Hairy Vetch, Australian Winter Peas,
Winter Rye, and some kind of clover,*
you said with triumph.

I can't wait to plow and seed!
You dig to show me eager soil.
I hear you have a new girlfriend too.

Open House

       She stares long into folds of red
draperies, the low ceilings

       of busy chambers, listens
to the oily gurgle and thump,

       thorough as a spy.
A year's passed since they inspected

       this tight-fisted home, its slick
sonorous walls. After years of constant

       checking, cutting, sewing, shocking,
my heart has tried to settle.

       But I can't seem to keep it to myself.
Most hearts go a lifetime keeping private

       schedules, love-struck and fear-smacked
secrets. But mine's been opened

       by those who pry, snoop
in drawers, shuffle the mail,

stop me,
                                    start me.

Leftover

Try my giblets, liver sauteed
in cognac and green peppercorns.

Careful with my heart,
take dainty bites around its metal bits,

aftermarket parts sewn in by surgeons,
built to last longer than I'll need.

You see the cook was distracted
when I was made, cooking left her bored.

Lost in her incessantly private thoughts
she burned the pan,

left my tender pieces seared and crumbly.
Once she dropped me

in the big pot, she found
the constant stirring insufferable,

the bouquet mismatched, tastes veering
from soggy fries to herbed chevre.

I was her stew that wouldn't mellow, a turmoil
of hairy carrots, kale, and stringy meat.

But now that the cook has thankfully quit,
take what you want, I've little need

of anything that was hers. I've softened,
a congenial leftover, ready to warm.

Dream: Common Crops

—Hopewell, New Jersey

First, I passed the cemetery
where my rebel ancestor rests.
Snow topped his tall obelisk
and spalled slab that stands
over the simple stones
of his neighbors.
His home and barns burned
to the ground in war.
He had so much
to lose.

Next, I found a garden
of common crops
still growing in the grip
of winter. The heart-shaped
leaves of lima beans encased
in ice, pods thick
as farmer's soles.
Here they grew,
defiantly enduring
February's clawing cold.

I held one leathery leaf
in my palm;
it was familiar
as the face of a friend.
Who remembers
the plain,
and necessary?
Who honors the quiet
ones who work
and can't surrender?

The Names Remain Unspoken

—for Sue

You write to tell me the names you find
picking your path over the hard hillocks
of a frozen New Hampshire cemetery.

We delight in names that haven't been heard
in centuries. Deliberate, plodding, fricative
strands of consonants rubbing frequent z's.

Sophronia. Azubah, Tryphena, Hezekiah.
And still the names remain unspoken;
you are alone besides the ticking chickadees.

From hundreds of miles away, my friend,
you send me this list of those assembled
with you. I think you miss these strangers,

as we miss each other, settled in the ways
that someday we too will enjoy, when our
supply of quiet days extends indefinitely.

Did You Pause?

—for my beloved teachers:
  Mary Edwards Shaner and Christopher Irwin Bursk

Did you pause, your thumb upon the latch,
to equivocate, to hold the memory of your love's face,
or was it clearly time?

Did you savor your slow suspension,
as a red rock balanced against an indigo sky,
no fear of crumbling on its fall?

I don't think you rushed into the jet night gleaming
ahead. I hope you coasted, the way a heron teases
the lake that waits to embrace it.

What It Is I Fear

> *She did not know what it was she feared,*
> *but it had to do with empty sardine cans in the sink.*
> —Joan Didion, *Play It as It Lays*

If you say *sink,*

>I see a silhouette who takes her dinner
>leaning over a drain.
>
>Or how to weep privately on an overnight flight.
>That woman's eyes a few rows back.

If you say *cans,*

>I remember faded labels at the dollar store, dented
>peaches, stew, and beans.
>
>Or a strand of tins warning of approaching
>newlyweds. A celebration that clanks.

If you say *sardines,*

>I think how a cannery crams cold fish together
>until they mold to each other's form.
>
>Or how a house constricts,
>unbreathable when the marriage ends.

If you say *empty,*

>that's when I know.

3

prepare

Longevity

My garden slumbers late
in the slow bake of August mornings.

Peppers wake, arch their glossy
backs and stretch into the scorched

white glare. Basil settles into cool roots to sip
from last night's downpour.

Tomatoes testify, push their hairy,
tin-scented arms skyward.

My garden is pell-mell, hotfoot, feverish,
sticky, stinking. It's all about the party.

There's no jittery murmur, no fear of maiming
grubs, only a sweet and salty gush.

And shouldn't this be the way, gorging
on sun and rain until we can't swallow another bite?

My garden has no time.

By September, stems are sucked dry,
branches broken, and vines snarled,

leaving only pumpkins that harden
in October's parched plot. They glow

as the very vines that bore them shrivel.
They hold hard to the short days,

determined to reap
some imagined reward.

"Bringing in the Sheaves"

—gospel song, Knowles Shaw, 1874

At the Mennonite thrift shop, I'm harvesting
old silk ties for a project.

Elbow deep, I feel around in musty mounds
of flannel shirts and quilted barn vests.

Ties settle to the bottom in groups, like snakes
snarled under matted straw.

Christian soft rock plays while the chaff
of Sunday dinners sheds into the air.

Now other shoppers hurl plaids, paisleys,
and regimental stripes into my pile.

Opening a bland gray tie, I find it's lined
with a pert photo of a puckered-up pinup.

I put it back,
giving it the chance to cause another stir.

We shall come rejoicing.

Hanging on the Gates

The resident raccoon knows heaven is hard
to reach. Learned he must climb

columns. Some hold seed, others offer the sweet
fat of suet swinging in cages. Every night he labors

with faith, until the metal welds surrender
and black oil seeds are heaved

in a midnight spread. Claws stuck
in the wire mesh, he once hung

nearly half an hour full believing
the latch would relent

and open to him once more. He understands
that heaven is only entered

with persistence.
He solemnly accepts,

we must apply each night.

The Blue Jay

Looks around, appraises his world, one slick black
oil seed clutched in his fierce beak. Berlin blue
sky. Flat, the blaze-white
winter sun flickers behind charcoal
trees casting streaks, indigo
bars, on lilac-gray
snow.

Today, the world matches
his expectations.

Forbidden Colors

Forbidden colors are composed of pairs of hues whose light frequencies automatically cancel each other out in the human eye.
—Natalie Wolchover, *Live Science*

The pool luxury
of sapphire
skies, buttercup
full-belly gold,

both light dispersed, segregated
by wavelengths.

We used to file colors
in separate
folders, as if one gender
owned them.

And so much talk
of color
fractures like ice
when we speak
of skin.

Physicists define *forbidden*
as a state that won't
conform.

They labor,
that we might perceive
red-green
or blue-yellow.

Those forbidden colors exist,
but their differences
align
in perfect opposition.

They leave a void
for want of our better vision.

Rare Beasts

The surface is broken
by my boat,
the hard heads
of turtles, fish stretching
their limits,
and dead branches
that have nothing left to defend.
Then a snake.
I understand
those better-safe-
than-sorry turtles leaping
from their logs; curious carp
that briefly visit our dimension.
But this snake,
this nonchalant
swimmer with such composure
decides that I'm
of no concern.
Yet my heart pounds,
as when holding my breath
for scans of my organs,
or listening for what to expect
while counting backwards.
So when do I get
that devil-may-care spirit,
the glassy eyes
of that scarce species that never worries?
Maybe that snake's heart
beat a little too fast
when he saw me coming.
And why do I hope that's true?
Our kind is always crashing

in the calm between two thorned
shores: the threat
we feel or the threat we are.
I raised my paddle high.

Fences Take

Here the land's been torn
then sewn into a quilt of plump

lawns and tight fences,
corrals for spaniels and retrievers.

Yesterday a doe and fawn crossed
the road into our yard, confined

by neighbors' fences on three sides.
What the doe jumped, entrapped

the fawn. She raced
back and forth for hours, panting.

We had to stop watching.

Today the morning chill is cut
by a shimmer of rank heat rising

from the one spot where the grass
is tall and grows freely.

Unstoppable

the moon's wordless drift

a chicken hellbent streaking for a fat beetle

the midnight banter of secrets between roof and rain

even the elderly

elms that line the road

will cross to the other side

after hosting the nurseries of squirrels

all that leafing and dropping

falling

the act they've rehearsed in their deepest heartwood

getting where we need to go

As One

Invited to a New Year's Eve party by a guy I barely knew,
I left my apartment late.

I was still riding the Green Line at midnight,
and nothing changed.

No celebration whoops or kisses, just lone travelers
closed up with our thoughts.

The cars rocked; our bodies swayed as one,
the way trees lean together in a storm.

Mortal Lessons

Back in the garden, I coo
for everyone in my best mother

voice. I'm sorry you all must grow
here. The best light is tight

up to the road where exhaust
and honking would stunt

lesser beings.
You are brave

while rodents gnaw
your reedy wood, run

roughshod over your home.
Scent of blood,

the tin musk of tomato limbs.
Here salvation smells

like a delivery room
in a war zone.

Caterpillars creep
up your legs

even as parasites drain
their green jelly.

Garden, you fight
despite my neglect

and the laws that force
one life to steal for another.

Feral Apples

Crowded by crabgrass
and roadside gravel,
they loll
where groundhogs graze
in peril. Their thick
skins yellow-streaked,
the north sun
too stingy to supply
a plush scarlet coat.

Those peels
hold a history
of pocks and pitted
scabs, left by maggot
flies, codling moths,
and fungus.
In autumn they swell
with fizzing fermentation
that draws the affection
of yellow jackets and deer.

Blowsy loiterers,
they canoodle, ooze
perfume, syrup,
and tumbles of ants
where anyone can see.
Inveterate urchins,
free to lounge
wherever they're spilled,
bitter, but too cunning
to resist.

They've so little
to give,
but there's always
someone ready to bite.

What Not to Cut

I try not to keep too much—bad
habits, the burdens of plans, jumble
and dross. But what to cut?

Busy today, no time for lunch. My jaw's
a little tight after a day at the office striving
to keep my mouth shut.

Somebody's aunt sent a box of peaches, onions,
and tomatoes. I filled a bag, while most were put off
by the mingling of sweet and stink.

The tomatoes sliced bleed
lavishly. The peaches bitten, dribble
sex and warmth.

But grand as a Dutch master, the cider-colored
onion glows, its smooth skin shining
ample in a low blue bowl.

Some things shouldn't be cut.

Feast

I love the fat of summer, flabby
green weeks when weeds lap

over the vague rims of back
roads, just as batter overtakes

a griddle. Poplar leaves wave
wide as cows' tongues slurping

syrup-thick air. Here, summer spits
when it talks, gulps cold milk

and wipes a hand across its mouth.
I want to stuff myself full

with warm fields, hills tender
and round as yeast rolls bathed

in butter. Oh to scoop the ooze
of June's soft eggs, consume

this season, lick its juices, chew
those salty bacon days,

until autumn clears
my plate.

Corn at Market

—after Mark Doty's "A Display of Mackerel"

Bundled together in a single bed like Chaucer's
pilgrims, ears of corn shiver in their emerald coats.

The market is freezing yet the top ones sweat. They suffer
the tampering that musses

their wiry brown hair as they shelter
the pale silk. Shoppers rip, tear,

strip them bare, and when finished
searching for perfection, toss most back.

All night the store lights bore into them.
Even sunlight's more forgiving.

Together they erect a pyramid to honor summer, built
to last no longer than a season.

They dream of home fields where the sun kicked
up a breeze and they swayed as one in a slow dance.

Long days when mice nibbled their necks,
not taking all that much.

On the bottom, they feel the weight, the dark safe
covering of kin. They hope for salvation

like anyone who's taken precarious cover, convinced
they won't be found. But they are.

And when we place them on our fires, their golden
spirits rise as steam.

They leave us to our anxious shuffling
as we wait to be the chosen ones.

Love Letter to My Garden

You are the mild earth under the searing sun.
You are mud or crumble.
You are futures for grubs and squash.
You are the tin scent of tomato arms, the furred faces of leaves.
You are a tangle of zucchini, the ambition of pumpkins.
You are the gleaming backs of peppers.
You are the incense of rosemary, the reverence of sage.

You are the kind of wealth I felt guilty about as a child.
You are the memory of my father, the descendent of his church.
You are my preacher, my Bach soaring from a skyward organ.
You are a place I never sit; I only stand or kneel.
You are the verve of my husband.
You are the hot red tulips he left in Haarlem.
You are the rising heat of my son at birth.

You welcome the wiry feet of robins who scratch your back.
You wind your limbs and gently sleep beside all who grow here.
You tolerate beating rain and the racket of storms.
You never steal land or water.
You won't spill blood.
You are new to me, yet old as stars.

Sweetness

A milk chocolate wren warms
the morning singing

allegro. Listening,
the cat's talkative tail dips

into honey meant for tea.
The brew cools while the chase

is on, as sweetness spreads
throughout my home.

Write to Me

If I wrote to you now, it would be no different
than a letter to that small house down by the park.
You know, the stucco cube with two dormers
built when the lake was an absentminded creek.

Now the house is empty. The reflected water
and honking of geese still bounce off its windows.
That old couple, who drove matching white cars
with Republican stickers, has moved out.

For days trucks jammed the driveway,
a dumpster sank into the muddy lawn,
heavy with smooth worn cabinets, well-walked
flooring, anything they could tear loose.

If the wife wrote a letter to the house,
she would see the salt and pepper still resting
on the table, her husband's latest issue
of TIME waiting on his recliner.

As I write to you now, I see you coming home
to stay and me showing you off as the prize
I won on your birthday. Write to me now,
my soldier son, tell me what you see.

November Reckons

November has stopped trying
to push that stray hair
behind her ear.

She's small now, small
as a musty apple
that's rolled

into the tall weeds.
On good days
she glows,

reflects the amber light
of an Old Master's varnish.
She bundles

her love
letters smelling of the dried
tea of summer,

studies her attic-scented
sweaters for signs
of the quiet

work of moths.
Other days, she soothes
her raw throat,

melts the first ice
of winter on her tongue.
November reckons,

weighs her choices:
the labor of reset or ease
of release.

She's Always Hungry

Winter arrives with the blank
face of a runway model, languid

and sheer as the chiffon scarf
that drifts across her shoulders.

Bored by the heat of living,
she abhors the goo and mess.

Old German named her
the time of water,

She makes my lake crack
and groan. That crisp

look she gives, so alluring
you'll ignore the chilly

clues of flat infatuation.
You don't stand a chance.

An empty retreat that never serves
meals; she wants us to learn

the difference between hunger
and greed. Praise the rare blue sky,

the weak brushstrokes of charcoal
trees, but don't fall for those sharp

bones that grin from under
her waxen skin. Prepare

a bed of crocuses, anxious
to spring from her grave.

About the Author

Jane Edna Mohler is author of *Broken Umbrellas* (Kelsay Books, 2019) and was the 2020 Bucks County Pennsylvania Poet Laureate. She won the 2016 Main Street Voices contest, placed second in the 2023 Crossroads Contest of the Eastern Shore Writers' Association, and was a finalist in the Robert Fraser Poetry Competition. Jane has been the Poetry Editor of the *Schuylkill Valley Journal* since 2021.

Jane had a long career as a counselor in many mental health settings, with most years consulting to a variety of k-12 schools. She also spent nearly two decades as an advocate for the educational rights of students experiencing homelessness. She was awarded a Fulbright Distinguished Award in Teaching but was unable to fulfill the honor due to a health emergency. When not writing or gardening, she is an American traditional rug hooker. She resides in Bucks County, Pennsylvania with her artist husband, Peter Stolvoort, and two very opinionated cats.

For more information, see:
janeednamohler.com